Where
the
Sidewalk
Ends

Where the Sidewalk Ends

the
poems
&
drawings
of
Shel Silverstein

PARTICULAR
BOOKS

PARTICULAR BOOKS

Published by the Penguin Group
Penguin Books Ltd, 80 Strand, London WC2R 0RL, England
Penguin Group (USA) Inc., 375 Hudson Street, New York, New York 10014, USA
Penguin Group (Canada), 90 Eglinton Avenue East, Suite 700, Toronto, Ontario, Canada M4P 2Y3
(a division of Pearson Penguin Canada Inc.)
Penguin Ireland, 25 St Stephen's Green, Dublin 2, Ireland (a division of Penguin Books Ltd)
Penguin Group (Australia), 250 Camberwell Road, Camberwell, Victoria 3124, Australia
(a division of Pearson Australia Group Pty Ltd)
Penguin Books India Pvt Ltd, 11 Community Centre, Panchsheel Park, New Delhi – 110 017, India
Penguin Group (NZ), 67 Apollo Drive, Rosedale, North Shore 0632, New Zealand
(a division of Pearson New Zealand Ltd)
Penguin Books (South Africa) (Pty) Ltd, 24 Sturdee Avenue, Rosebank, Johannesburg 2196, South Africa

Penguin Books Ltd, Registered Offices: 80 Strand, London WC2R 0RL, England

www.penguin.com

First published 1974
Published in Particular Books 2010
10

Printed and bound in Great Britain by TJ International Ltd.

A CIP catalogue record for this book is available from the British Library

978-1-846-14384-7

www.greenpenguin.co.uk

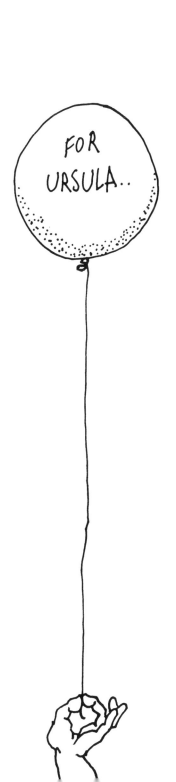

Where the Sidewalk Ends

INVITATION

If you are a dreamer, come in,
If you are a dreamer, a wisher, a liar,
A hope-er, a pray-er, a magic bean buyer . . .
If you're a pretender, come sit by my fire
For we have some flax-golden tales to spin.
Come in!
Come in!

THE ACROBATS

I'll swing
By my ankles,
She'll cling
To your knees
As you hang
By your nose
From a high-up
Trapeze.
But just one thing, please,
As we float through the breeze—
Don't sneeze.

MAGIC

Sandra's seen a leprechaun,
Eddie touched a troll,
Laurie danced with witches once,
Charlie found some goblins' gold.
Donald heard a mermaid sing,
Susy spied an elf,
But all the magic I have known
I've had to make myself.

HOMEMADE BOAT

This boat that we just built is just fine—
And don't try to tell us it's not.
The sides and the back are divine—
It's the bottom I guess we forgot. . . .

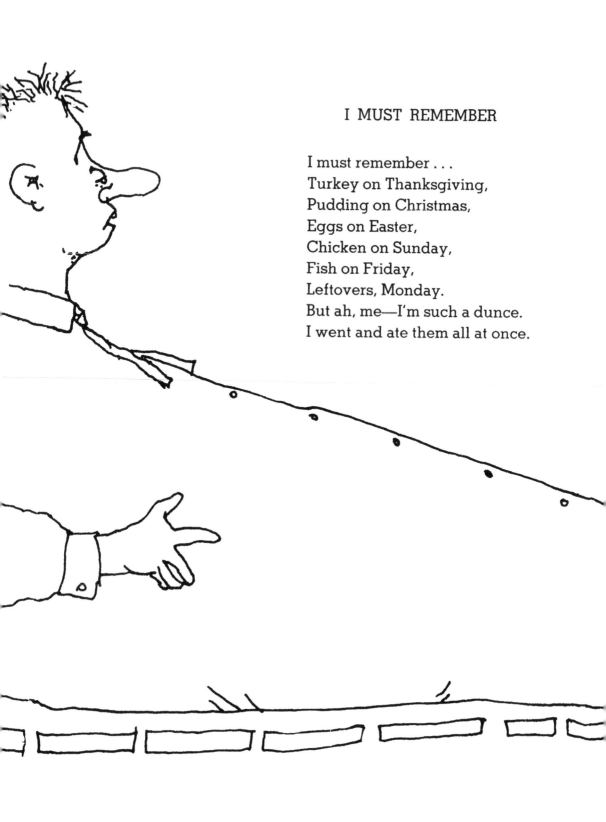

I MUST REMEMBER

I must remember . . .
Turkey on Thanksgiving,
Pudding on Christmas,
Eggs on Easter,
Chicken on Sunday,
Fish on Friday,
Leftovers, Monday.
But ah, me—I'm such a dunce.
I went and ate them all at once.

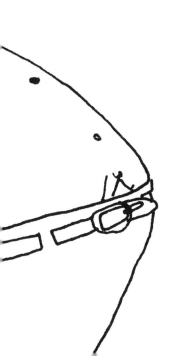

THE FOURTH

Oh
CRASH!
my
BASH!
it's
BANG!
the
ZANG!
Fourth
WHOOSH!
of
BAROOOM!
July
WHEW!

ICKLE ME, PICKLE ME, TICKLE ME TOO

Ickle Me, Pickle Me, Tickle Me too
Went for a ride in a flying shoe.
"Hooray!"
"What fun!"
"It's time we flew!"
Said Ickle Me, Pickle Me, Tickle Me too.

Ickle was captain, and Pickle was crew
And Tickle served coffee and mulligan stew
As higher
And higher
And higher they flew,
Ickle Me, Pickle Me, Tickle Me too.

Ickle Me, Pickle Me, Tickle Me too,
Over the sun and beyond the blue.
"Hold on!"
"Stay in!"
"I hope we do!"
Cried Ickle Me, Pickle Me, Tickle Me too.

Ickle Me, Pickle Me, Tickle Me too
Never returned to the world they knew,
And nobody
Knows what's
Happened to
Dear Ickle Me, Pickle Me, Tickle Me too.

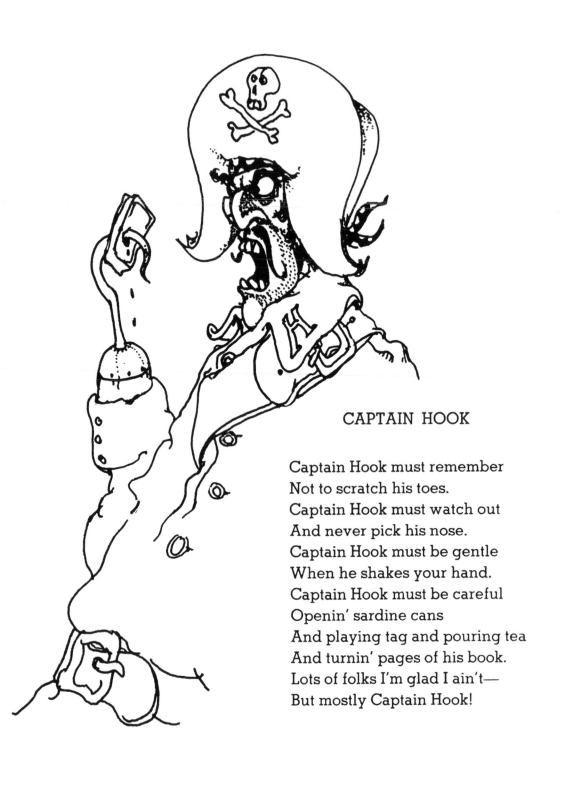

CAPTAIN HOOK

Captain Hook must remember
Not to scratch his toes.
Captain Hook must watch out
And never pick his nose.
Captain Hook must be gentle
When he shakes your hand.
Captain Hook must be careful
Openin' sardine cans
And playing tag and pouring tea
And turnin' pages of his book.
Lots of folks I'm glad I ain't—
But mostly Captain Hook!

HUG O' WAR

I will not play at tug o' war.
I'd rather play at hug o' war,
Where everyone hugs
Instead of tugs,
Where everyone giggles
And rolls on the rug,
Where everyone kisses,
And everyone grins,
And everyone cuddles,
And everyone wins.

IT'S DARK IN HERE

I am writing these poems
From inside a lion,
And it's rather dark in here.
So please excuse the handwriting
Which may not be too clear.
But this afternoon by the lion's cage
I'm afraid I got too near.
And I'm writing these lines
From inside a lion,
And it's rather dark in here.

OURCHESTRA

So you haven't got a drum, just beat your belly.
So I haven't got a horn—I'll play my nose.
So we haven't any cymbals—
We'll just slap our hands together,
And though there may be orchestras
That sound a little better
With their fancy shiny instruments
That cost an awful lot—
Hey, we're making music twice as good
By playing what we've got!

FLAG

One star is for Alaska . . .
One star is for Nebraska . . .
One star is North Dakota . . .
One star is Minnesota . . .
There are lots of other stars,
But I forget which ones they are.

COLORS

My skin is kind of sort of brownish
Pinkish yellowish white.
My eyes are greyish blueish green,
But I'm told they look orange in the night.
My hair is reddish blondish brown,
But it's silver when it's wet.
And all the colors I am inside
Have not been invented yet.

THE LOSER

Mama said I'd lose my head
If it wasn't fastened on.
Today I guess it wasn't
'Cause while playing with my cousin
It fell off and rolled away
And now it's gone.

And I can't look for it
'Cause my eyes are in it,
And I can't call to it
'Cause my mouth is on it
(Couldn't hear me anyway
'Cause my ears are on it),
Can't even think about it
'Cause my brain is in it.
So I guess I'll sit down
On this rock
And rest for just a minute....

JOEY

Joey Joey took a stone
And knocked
Down
The
Sun!
And whoosh! it swizzled
Down so hard,
And bloomp! it bounced
In his backyard,
And glunk! it landed
On his toe!
And the world was dark,
And the corn wouldn't grow,
And the wind wouldn't blow,
And the cock wouldn't crow,
And it always was Night,
Night,
Night.

All because
Of a stone
And Joe.

LISTEN TO THE MUSTN'TS

Listen to the MUSTN'TS, child,
Listen to the DON'TS
Listen to the SHOULDN'TS
The IMPOSSIBLES, the WON'TS
Listen to the NEVER HAVES
Then listen close to me—
Anything can happen, child,
ANYTHING can be.

JIMMY JET AND HIS TV SET

I'll tell you the story of Jimmy Jet—
And you know what I tell you is true.
He loved to watch his TV set
Almost as much as you.

He watched all day, he watched all night
Till he grew pale and lean,
From "The Early Show" to "The Late Late Show"
And all the shows between.

He watched till his eyes were frozen wide,
And his bottom grew into his chair.
And his chin turned into a tuning dial,
And antennae grew out of his hair.

And his brains turned into TV tubes,
And his face to a TV screen.
And two knobs saying "VERT." and "HORIZ."
Grew where his ears had been.

And he grew a plug that looked like a tail
So we plugged in little Jim.
And now instead of him watching TV
We all sit around and watch him.

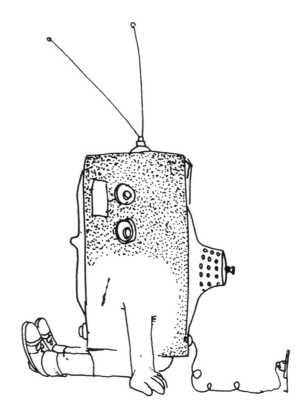

EARLY BIRD

Oh, if you're a bird, be an early bird
And catch the worm for your breakfast plate.
If you're a bird, be an early early bird—
But if you're a worm, sleep late.

SKY SEASONING

A piece of sky
Broke off and fell
Through the crack in the ceiling
Right into my soup,
KERPLOP!
I really must state
That I usually hate
Lentil soup, but I ate
Every drop!
Delicious delicious
(A bit like plaster),
But so delicious, goodness sake—
I could have eaten a lentil-soup lake.
It's amazing the difference
A bit of sky can make.

THE FARMER AND THE QUEEN

"She's coming," the farmer said to the owl.
"Oh, what shall I, what shall I do?
Shall I bow when she comes?
Shall I twiddle my thumbs?"
    The owl asked, "Who?"

"The Queen, the Queen, the royal Queen—
She'll pass the farm today.
Shall I salute?" he asked the horse.
    The horse said, "Nay."

"Shall I give her a gift?" he asked the wren.
"A lovely memento for her to keep?
An egg or a peach or an ear of corn?"
    The wren said, "Cheap."

"But should I curtsy or should I cheer?
Oh, here's her carriage now.
What should I do?" he asked the dog.
    The dog said, "Bow."

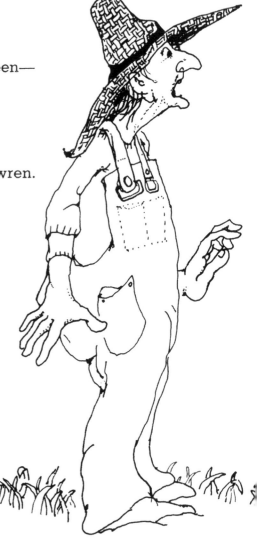

And so he did, and so she passed,
Oh, tra lala lala,
"She smiled, she did!" he told the sheep.
    The sheep said, "Bah."

PANCAKE?

Who wants a pancake,
Sweet and piping hot?
Good little Grace looks up and says,
"I'll take the one on top."
Who else wants a pancake,
Fresh off the griddle?
Terrible Theresa smiles and says,
"I'll take the one in the middle."

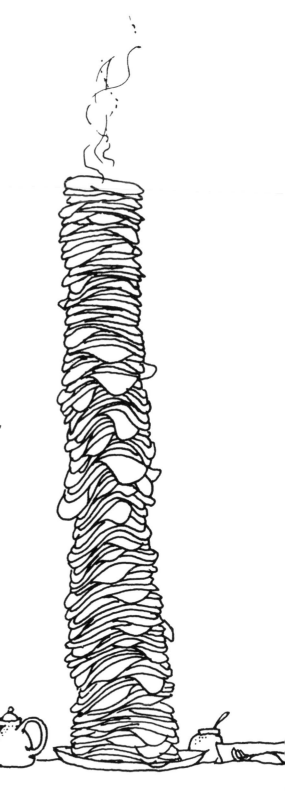

SMART

My dad gave me one dollar bill
'Cause I'm his smartest son,
And I swapped it for two shiny quarters
'Cause two is more than one!

And then I took the quarters
And traded them to Lou
For three dimes—I guess he don't know
That three is more than two!

Just then, along came old blind Bates
And just 'cause he can't see
He gave me four nickels for my three dimes,
And four is more than three!

And I took the nickels to Hiram Coombs
Down at the seed-feed store,
And the fool gave me five pennies for them,
And five is more than four!

And then I went and showed my dad,
And he got red in the cheeks
And closed his eyes and shook his head—
Too proud of me to speak!

US

Me and him
Him and me,
We're always together
As you can see.
I wish he'd leave
So I'd be free
I'm getting a little bit
Tired of he,
And he may be a bit
Bored with me.
On movies and ladies
We cannot agree.
I like to dance
He loves to ski.
He likes the mountains
I love the sea.
I like hot chocolate
He wants his tea.
I want to sleep
He has to pee.
He's meaner and duller
And fatter than me.
But I guess there's worse things
We could be—
Instead of two we could be three,
Me and him
Him and me.

36

I'M MAKING A LIST

I'm making a list of the things I must say
        for politeness,
And goodness and kindness and gentleness,
      sweetness and rightness:
          Hello
          Pardon me
          How are you?
          Excuse me
          Bless you
          May I?
          Thank you
          Goodbye
If you know some that I've forgot,
    please stick them in your eye!

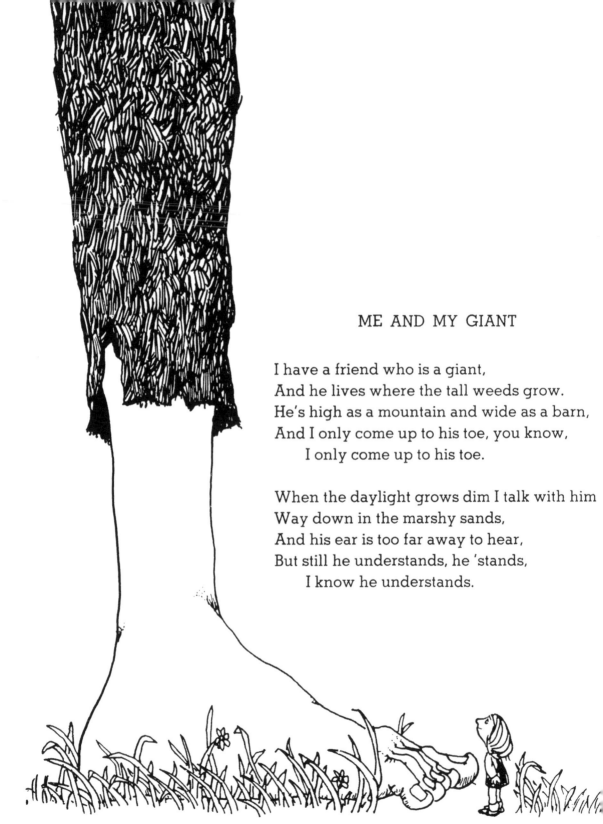

ME AND MY GIANT

I have a friend who is a giant,
And he lives where the tall weeds grow.
He's high as a mountain and wide as a barn,
And I only come up to his toe, you know,
    I only come up to his toe.

When the daylight grows dim I talk with him
Way down in the marshy sands,
And his ear is too far away to hear,
But still he understands, he 'stands,
    I know he understands.

For we have a code called the "scratch-tap code,"
And here is what we do—
I scratch his toe . . . once means, "Hello"
And twice means, "How are you?"
Three means, "Does it look like rain?"
Four times means, "Don't cry."
Five times means, "I'll scratch you a joke."
And six times means, "Goodbye," "Goodbye,"
    Six times means, "Goodbye."

And he answers me by tapping his toe—
Once means, "Hello, friend."
Two taps means, "It's very nice to feel your scratch again."
Three taps means, "It's lonely here
With my head in the top of the sky."
Four taps means, "Today an eagle smiled as she flew by."
Five taps means, "Oops, I just bumped
    my head against the moon."
Six means, "Sigh" and seven means, "Bye"
And eight means, "Come back soon, soon, soon,"
    Eight means, "Come back soon."

And then I scratch a thousand times,
And he taps with a bappity-bimm,
And he laughs so hard he shakes the sky—
    That means I'm tickling him!

RAIN

I opened my eyes
And looked up at the rain,
And it dripped in my head
And flowed into my brain,
And all that I hear as I lie in my bed
Is the slishity-slosh of the rain in my head.

I step very softly,
I walk very slow,
I can't do a handstand—
I might overflow,
So pardon the wild crazy thing I just said—
I'm just not the same since there's rain in my head.

TWO BOXES

Two boxes met upon the road.
Said one unto the other,
"If you're a box,
And I'm a box,
Then you must be my brother.
Our sides are thin,
We're cavin' in,
And we must get no thinner."
And so two boxes, hand in hand,
Went home to have their dinner.

TRUE STORY

This morning I jumped on my horse
And went out for a ride,
And some wild outlaws chased me
And they shot me in the side.
So I crawled into a wildcat's cave
To find a place to hide,
But some pirates found me sleeping there,
And soon they had me tied
To a pole and built a fire
Under me—I almost cried
Till a mermaid came and cut me loose
And begged to be my bride,
So I said I'd come back Wednesday
But I must admit I lied.
Then I ran into a jungle swamp
But I forgot my guide
And I stepped into some quicksand,
And no matter how I tried
I couldn't get out, until I met
A water snake named Clyde,
Who pulled me to some cannibals
Who planned to have me fried.
But an eagle came and swooped me up
And through the air we flied,
But he dropped me in a boiling lake
A thousand miles wide.
And you'll never guess what I did then—
I DIED.

BOA CONSTRICTOR

Oh, I'm being eaten
By a boa constrictor,
A boa constrictor,
A boa constrictor,
I'm being eaten by a boa constrictor,
And I don't like it—one bit.
Well, what do you know?
It's nibblin' my toe.
Oh, gee,
It's up to my knee.
Oh my,
It's up to my thigh.
Oh, fiddle,
It's up to my middle.
Oh, heck,
It's up to my neck.
Oh, dread,
It's upmmmmmmmmmmmfffffffffff. . .

HECTOR THE COLLECTOR

Hector the Collector
Collected bits of string,
Collected dolls with broken heads
And rusty bells that would not ring.
Pieces out of picture puzzles,
Bent-up nails and ice-cream sticks,
Twists of wires, worn-out tires,
Paper bags and broken bricks.

Old chipped vases, half shoelaces,
Gatlin' guns that wouldn't shoot,
Leaky boats that wouldn't float
And stopped-up horns that wouldn't toot.
Butter knives that had no handles,
Copper keys that fit no locks,
Rings that were too small for fingers,
Dried-up leaves and patched-up socks.
Worn-out belts that had no buckles,
'Lectric trains that had no tracks,
Airplane models, broken bottles,
Three-legged chairs and cups with cracks.
Hector the Collector
Loved these things with all his soul—
Loved them more than shining diamonds,
Loved them more than glistenin' gold.
Hector called to all the people,
"Come and share my treasure trunk!"
And all the silly sightless people
Came and looked . . . and called it junk.

INVENTION

I've done it, I've done it!
Guess what I've done!
Invented a light that plugs into the sun.
The sun is bright enough,
The bulb is strong enough,
But, oh, there's only one thing wrong . . .

The cord ain't long enough.

THE GOOGIES ARE COMING

The googies are coming, the old people say,
To buy little children and take them away.
Fifty cents for fat ones,
Twenty cents for lean ones,
Fifteen cents for dirty ones,
Thirty cents for clean ones,
A nickel each for mean ones.

The googies are coming, and maybe tonight,
To buy little children and lock them up tight.
Eighty cents for husky ones,
Quarter for the weak ones,
Penny each for noisy ones,
A dollar for the meek ones.

Forty cents for happy ones,
Eleven cents for sad ones.
And, kiddies, when they come to buy,
It won't do any good to cry.
But—just between yourself and I—
They never buy the bad ones!

FOR SALE

One sister for sale!
One sister for sale!
One crying and spying young sister for sale!
I'm really not kidding,
So who'll start the bidding?
Do I hear a dollar?
A nickel?
A penny?
Oh, isn't there, isn't there, isn't there any
One kid who will buy this old sister for sale,
This crying and spying young sister for sale?

SLEEPING SARDINES

"I'm tired of eating just beans," says I,
So I opened a can of sardines.
But they started to squeak,
"Hey, we're tryin' to sleep.
We were snuggled up tight
Till you let in the light.
You big silly sap, let us finish our nap.
Now close up the lid!"
So that's what I did. . . .
Will somebody please pass the beans?

ONE INCH TALL

If you were only one inch tall, you'd ride a worm to school.
The teardrop of a crying ant would be your swimming pool.
A crumb of cake would be a feast
And last you seven days at least,
A flea would be a frightening beast
If you were one inch tall.

If you were only one inch tall, you'd walk beneath the door,
And it would take about a month to get down to the store.
A bit of fluff would be your bed,
You'd swing upon a spider's thread,
And wear a thimble on your head
If you were one inch tall.

You'd surf across the kitchen sink upon a stick of gum.
You couldn't hug your mama, you'd just have to hug her thumb.
You'd run from people's feet in fright,
To move a pen would take all night,
(This poem took fourteen years to write—
'Cause I'm just one inch tall).

ENTER THIS DESERTED HOUSE

But please walk softly as you do.
Frogs dwell here and crickets too.

Ain't no ceiling, only blue
Jays dwell here and sunbeams too.

Floors are flowers—take a few.
Ferns grow here and daisies too.

Whoosh, swoosh—too-whit, too-woo,
Bats dwell here and hoot owls too.

Ha-ha-ha, hee-hee, hoo-hoooo,
Gnomes dwell here and goblins too.

And my child, I thought you knew
I dwell here . . . and so do you.

SICK

"I cannot go to school today,"
Said little Peggy Ann McKay.
"I have the measles and the mumps,
A gash, a rash and purple bumps.
My mouth is wet, my throat is dry,
I'm going blind in my right eye.
My tonsils are as big as rocks,
I've counted sixteen chicken pox
And there's one more—that's seventeen,
And don't you think my face looks green?
My leg is cut, my eyes are blue—
It might be instamatic flu.
I cough and sneeze and gasp and choke,
I'm sure that my left leg is broke—

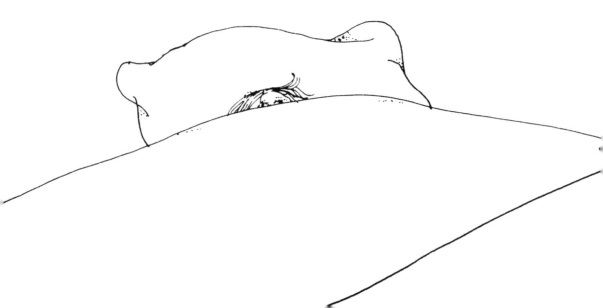

My hip hurts when I move my chin,
My belly button's caving in,
My back is wrenched, my ankle's sprained,
My 'pendix pains each time it rains.
My nose is cold, my toes are numb,
I have a sliver in my thumb.
My neck is stiff, my voice is weak,
I hardly whisper when I speak.
My tongue is filling up my mouth,
I think my hair is falling out.
My elbow's bent, my spine ain't straight,
My temperature is one-o-eight.
My brain is shrunk, I cannot hear,
There is a hole inside my ear.
I have a hangnail, and my heart is—what?
What's that? What's that you say?
You say today is . . . Saturday?
G'bye, I'm going out to play!"

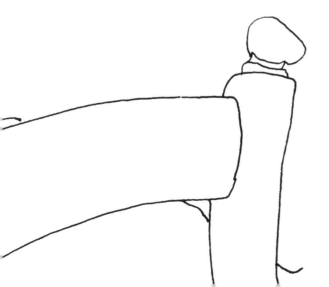

UPSTAIRS

There's a family of wrens who live upstairs,
Upstairs, upstairs, upstairs,
Inside my hat, all cozy in
My hair, my hair, my hair.
I've moved a dozen times and still
They're there, they're there, they're there.
I'd like to get away from them,
But where, but where, but where?
This hat just isn't big enough
To share, to share, to share.
But now I see you're bored and you
Don't care, don't care, don't care
'Bout the wrens who live inside
My hair, my hair, my hair.

THE GARDEN

Ol' man Simon, planted a diamond,
Grew hisself a garden the likes of none.
Sprouts all growin', comin' up glowin',
Fruit of jewels all shinin' in the sun.
Colors of the rainbow,
See the sun and rain grow
Sapphires and rubies on ivory vines,
Grapes of jade, just
Ripenin' in the shade, just
Ready for the squeezin' into green jade wine.
Pure gold corn there,
Blowin' in the warm air,
Ol' crow nibblin' on the amnythyst seeds.
In between the diamonds, ol' man Simon
Crawls about pullin' out platinum weeds.
Pink pearl berries,
All you can carry,
Put 'em in a bushel and
Haul 'em into town.
Up in the tree there's
Opal nuts and gold pears—
Hurry quick, grab a stick
And shake some down.
Take a silver tater,
Emerald tomater,
Fresh plump coral melons
Hangin' in reach.
Ol' man Simon,
Diggin' in his diamonds,
Stops and rests and dreams about
One . . . real . . . peach.

JUMPING ROPE

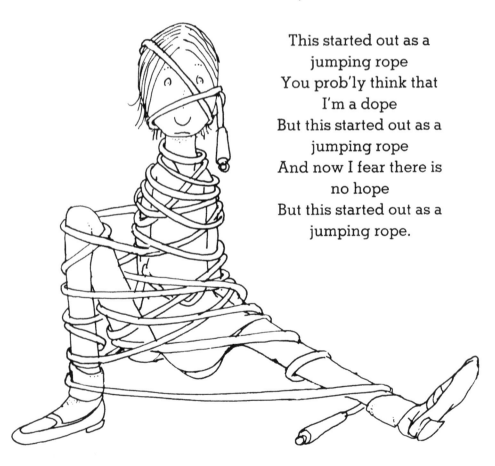

This started out as a
jumping rope
You prob'ly think that
I'm a dope
But this started out as a
jumping rope
And now I fear there is
no hope
But this started out as a
jumping rope.

WHO

Who can kick a football
From here out to Afghanistan?
I can!
Who fought tigers in the street
While all the policemen ran and hid?
I did!
Who will fly and have X-ray eyes—
And be known as the man no bullet can kill?
I will!
Who can sit and tell lies all night?
I might!

RIDICULOUS ROSE

Her mama said, "Don't eat with your fingers."
"OK," said Ridiculous Rose,
So she ate with her toes!

WHERE THE SIDEWALK ENDS

There is a place where the sidewalk ends
And before the street begins,
And there the grass grows soft and white,
And there the sun burns crimson bright,
And there the moon-bird rests from his flight
To cool in the peppermint wind.

Let us leave this place where the smoke blows black
And the dark street winds and bends.
Past the pits where the asphalt flowers grow
We shall walk with a walk that is measured and slow,
And watch where the chalk-white arrows go
To the place where the sidewalk ends.

Yes we'll walk with a walk that is measured and slow,
And we'll go where the chalk-white arrows go,
For the children, they mark, and the children, they know
The place where the sidewalk ends.

SNOWMAN

'Twas the first day of the springtime,
And the snowman stood alone
As the winter snows were melting,
And the pine trees seemed to groan,
"Ah, you poor sad smiling snowman,
You'll be melting by and by."
Said the snowman, "What a pity,
For I'd like to see July.
Yes, I'd like to see July, and please don't ask me why.
But I'd like to, yes I'd like to, oh I'd like to see July."

Chirped a robin, just arriving,
"Seasons come and seasons go,
And the greatest ice must crumble
When it's flowers' time to grow.
And as one thing is beginning
So another thing must die,
And there's never been a snowman
Who has ever seen July.
No, they never see July, no matter how they try.
No, they never ever, never ever, never see July."

But the snowman sniffed his carrot nose
And said, "At least I'll try,"
And he bravely smiled his frosty smile
And blinked his coal-black eye.
And there he stood and faced the sun
A blazin' from the sky—
And I really cannot tell you
If he ever saw July.
Did he ever see July? You can guess as well as I
If he ever, if he never, if he ever saw July.

THE CROCODILE'S TOOTHACHE

The Crocodile
Went to the dentist
And sat down in the chair,
And the dentist said, "Now tell me, sir,
Why does it hurt and where?"
And the Crocodile said, "I'll tell you the truth,
I have a terrible ache in my tooth,"
And he opened his jaws so wide, so wide,
That the dentist, he climbed right inside,
And the dentist laughed, "Oh isn't this fun?"
As he pulled the teeth out, one by one.
And the Crocodile cried, "You're hurting me so!
Please put down your pliers and let me go."
But the dentist just laughed with a Ho Ho Ho,
And he said, "I still have twelve to go—
Oops, that's the wrong one, I confess,
But what's one crocodile's tooth, more or less?"
Then suddenly, the jaws went SNAP,
And the dentist was gone, right off the map,
And where he went one could only guess . . .
To North or South or East or West . . .
He left no forwarding address.
But what's one dentist, more or less?

THUMBS

Oh the thumb-sucker's thumb
May look wrinkled and wet
And withered, and white as the snow,
But the taste of a thumb
Is the sweetest taste yet
(As only we thumb-suckers know).

WILD BOAR

If you tell me the wild boar
Has twenty teeth, I'll say, "Why shore."
Or say that he has thirty-three,
That number's quite all right with me.
Or scream that he has ninety-nine,
I'll never say that you are lyin',
For the number of teeth
In a wild boar's mouth
Is a subject I'm glad
I know nothing abouth.

LESTER

Lester was given a magic wish
By the goblin who lives in the banyan tree,
And with his wish he wished for two more wishes—
So now instead of just one wish, he cleverly had three.
And with each one of these
He simply wished for three more wishes,
Which gave him three old wishes, plus nine new.
And with each of these twelve
He slyly wished for three more wishes,
Which added up to forty-six—or is it fifty-two?
Well anyway, he used each wish
To wish for wishes 'til he had
Five billion, seven million, eighteen thousand thirty-four.
And then he spread them on the ground
And clapped his hands and danced around
And skipped and sang, and then sat down
And wished for more.
And more . . . and more . . . they multiplied
While other people smiled and cried
And loved and reached and touched and felt.
Lester sat amid his wealth
Stacked mountain-high like stacks of gold,
Sat and counted—and grew old.
And then one Thursday night they found him
Dead—with his wishes piled around him.
And they counted the lot and found that not
A single one was missing.
All shiny and new—here, take a few
And think of Lester as you do.
In a world of apples and kisses and shoes
He wasted his wishes on wishing.

SARAH CYNTHIA SYLVIA STOUT
WOULD NOT TAKE THE GARBAGE OUT

Sarah Cynthia Sylvia Stout
Would not take the garbage out!
She'd scour the pots and scrape the pans,
Candy the yams and spice the hams,
And though her daddy would scream and shout,
She simply would not take the garbage out.
And so it piled up to the ceilings:
Coffee grounds, potato peelings,
Brown bananas, rotten peas,
Chunks of sour cottage cheese.
It filled the can, it covered the floor,
It cracked the window and blocked the door
With bacon rinds and chicken bones,
Drippy ends of ice cream cones,
Prune pits, peach pits, orange peel,
Gloppy glumps of cold oatmeal,
Pizza crusts and withered greens,
Soggy beans and tangerines,
Crusts of black burned buttered toast,
Gristly bits of beefy roasts . . .
The garbage rolled on down the hall,
It raised the roof, it broke the wall . . .

Greasy napkins, cookie crumbs,
Globs of gooey bubble gum,
Cellophane from green baloney,
Rubbery blubbery macaroni,
Peanut butter, caked and dry,
Curdled milk and crusts of pie,
Moldy melons, dried-up mustard,
Eggshells mixed with lemon custard,
Cold french fries and rancid meat,
Yellow lumps of Cream of Wheat.
At last the garbage reached so high
That finally it touched the sky.
And all the neighbors moved away,
And none of her friends would come to play.
And finally Sarah Cynthia Stout said,
"OK, I'll take the garbage out!"
But then, of course, it was too late . . .
The garbage reached across the state,
From New York to the Golden Gate.
And there, in the garbage she did hate,
Poor Sarah met an awful fate,
That I cannot right now relate
Because the hour is much too late.
But children, remember Sarah Stout
And always take the garbage out!

DRATS

Can anyone lend me
Two eighty-pound rats?
I want to rid my house of cats.

HAT

Teddy said it was a hat,
So I put it on.
Now Dad is saying,
"Where the heck's
   the toilet plunger gone?"

MY RULES

If you want to marry me, here's what you'll have to do:
You must learn how to make a perfect chicken-dumpling stew.
And you must sew my holey socks,
And soothe my troubled mind,
And develop the knack for scratching my back,
And keep my shoes spotlessly shined.
And while I rest you must rake up the leaves,
And when it is hailing and snowing
You must shovel the walk . . . and be still when I talk,
And—hey—where are you going?

OH HAVE YOU HEARD

Oh have you heard it's time for vaccinations?
I think someone put salt into your tea.
They're giving us eleven-month vacations.
And Florida has sunk into the sea.

Oh have you heard the President has measles?
The principal has just burned down the school.
Your hair is full of ants and purple weasels—
            APRIL FOOL!

WARNING

Inside everybody's nose
There lives a sharp-toothed snail.
So if you stick your finger in,
He may bite off your nail.
Stick it farther up inside,
And he may bite your ring off.
Stick it all the way, and he
May bite the whole darn thing off.

THE UNICORN

A long time ago, when the earth was green
And there was more kinds of animals than you've ever seen,
And they run around free while the world was bein' born,
And the loveliest of all was the Unicorn.
    There was green alligators and long-neck geese.
    There was humpy bumpy camels and chimpanzees.
    There was catsandratsandelephants, but sure as you're born
    The loveliest of all was the Unicorn.

But the Lord seen some sinnin', and it caused him pain.
He says, "Stand back, I'm gonna make it rain."
He says, "Hey Brother Noah, I'll tell ya whatcha do.
Go and build me a floatin' zoo.
    And you take two alligators, and a couple of geese,
    Two humpy bumpy camels and two chimpanzees.
    Take two catsandratsandelephants, but sure as you're born
    Noah, don't you forget my Unicorn."

Now Noah was there, and he answered the callin',
And he finished up the ark just as the rain started fallin'.
He marched in the animals two by two,
And he called out as they went through,
    "Hey Lord, I got your two alligators and your couple of geese,
    Your humpy bumpy camels and your two chimpanzees.
    Got your catsandratsandelephants—but Lord, I'm so forlorn
    'Cause I just don't see no Unicorn."

Ol' Noah looked out through the drivin' rain,
But the Unicorns were hidin', playin' silly games.
They were kickin' and splashin' in the misty morn,
Oh them silly Unicorn.
 Then the goat started goatin', and the snake started snakin',
 The elephant started elephantin', and the boat started shakin'.
 The mouse started squeakin', and the lion started roarin',
 And everyone's aboard but the Unicorn.
 I mean the green alligators and the long-neck geese,
 The humpy bumpy camels and the chimpanzees.
 Noah cried, "Close the door 'cause the rain is pourin'—
 And we just can't wait for them Unicorn."

Then the ark started movin', and it drifted with the tide,
And the Unicorns looked up from the rock and cried.
And the water come up and sort of floated them away—
That's why you've never seen a Unicorn to this day.
 You'll see a lot of alligators and a whole mess of geese.
 You'll see humpy bumpy camels and lots of chimpanzees.
 You'll see catsandratsandelephants, but sure as you're born
 You're never gonna see no Unicorn.

TREE HOUSE

A tree house, a free house,
A secret you and me house,
A high up in the leafy branches
Cozy as can be house.

A street house, a neat house,
Be sure and wipe your feet house
Is not my kind of house at all—
Let's go live in a tree house.

THE FLYING FESTOON

Oh I'm going to ride on The Flying Festoon—
I'll jump on his back and I'll whistle a tune,
And we'll fly to the outermost tip of the moon,
      The Flying Festoon and I.

I'm taking a sandwich, and ball and a prune,
And we're leaving this evening precisely at noon,
For I'm going to fly with The Flying Festoon . . .
      Just as soon as he learns how to fly.

NO DIFFERENCE

Small as a peanut,
Big as a giant,
We're all the same size
When we turn off the light.

Rich as a sultan,
Poor as a mite,
We're all worth the same
When we turn off the light.

Red, black or orange,
Yellow or white,
We all look the same
When we turn off the light.

So maybe the way
To make everything right
Is for God to just reach out
And turn off the light!

INVISIBLE BOY

And here we see the invisible boy
In his lovely invisible house,
Feeding a piece of invisible cheese
To a little invisible mouse.
Oh, what a beautiful picture to see!
Will you draw an invisible picture for me?

TIGHT HAT

I tried to tip my hat to Miss McGaffry,
I never should have put it on so tight,
'Cause it wouldn't come off my head
And my neck got stretched instead.
That's what you get for tryin'
To be polite.

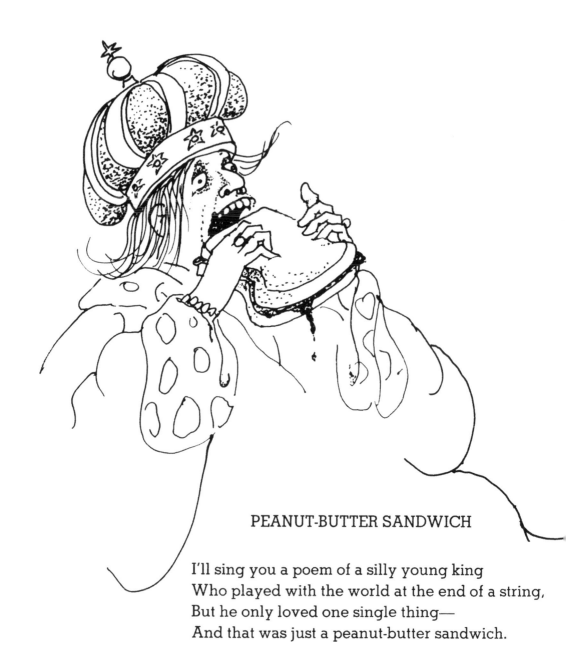

PEANUT-BUTTER SANDWICH

I'll sing you a poem of a silly young king
Who played with the world at the end of a string,
But he only loved one single thing—
And that was just a peanut-butter sandwich.

His scepter and his royal gowns,
His regal throne and golden crowns
Were brown and sticky from the mounds
And drippings from each peanut-butter sandwich.

His subjects all were silly fools
For he had passed a royal rule
That all that they could learn in school
Was how to make a peanut-butter sandwich.

He would not eat his sovereign steak,
He scorned his soup and kingly cake,
And told his courtly cook to bake
An extra-sticky peanut-butter sandwich.

And then one day he took a bite
And started chewing with delight,
But found his mouth was stuck quite tight
From that last bite of peanut-butter sandwich.

His brother pulled, his sister pried,
The wizard pushed, his mother cried,
"My boy's committed suicide
From eating his last peanut-butter sandwich!"

The dentist came, and the royal doc.
The royal plumber banged and knocked,
But still those jaws stayed tightly locked.
Oh darn that sticky peanut-butter sandwich!

The carpenter, he tried with pliers,
The telephone man tried with wires,
The firemen, they tried with fire,
But couldn't melt that peanut-butter sandwich.

With ropes and pulleys, drills and coil,
With steam and lubricating oil—
For twenty years of tears and toil—
They fought that awful peanut-butter sandwich.

Then all his royal subjects came.
They hooked his jaws with grapplin' chains
And pulled both ways with might and main
Against that stubborn peanut-butter sandwich.

Each man and woman, girl and boy
Put down their ploughs and pots and toys
And pulled until kerack! Oh, joy—
They broke right through that peanut-butter sandwich.

A puff of dust, a screech, a squeak—
The king's jaw opened with a creak.
And then in voice so faint and weak—
The first words that they heard him speak
Were, "How about a peanut-butter sandwich?"

LAZY JANE

Lazy
lazy
lazy
lazy
lazy
lazy
Jane,
she
wants
a
drink
of
water
so
she
waits
and
waits
and
waits
and
waits
and
waits
for
it
to
rain.

THE EDGE OF THE WORLD

Columbus said the world is round?
Don't you believe a word of that.
For I've been down to the edge of the world,
Sat on the edge where the wild wind whirled,
Peeked over the ledge where the blue smoke curls,
And I can tell you, boys and girls,
The world is FLAT!

SANTA AND THE REINDEER

"This is the hour," said Santa Claus,
"The bells ring merrily."
Then on his back he slung his pack,
And into his sleigh climbed he.

"On, Dancer! On, Prancer! On, Donner and Blitzen!
On, Comet and Cupid!" cried he.
And all the reindeers leaped but one,
And that one stood silently.

He had pulled the sleigh for a thousand years,
And never a word spoke he.
Now he stood in the snow, and he whispered low—
"Oh what do you have for me?"

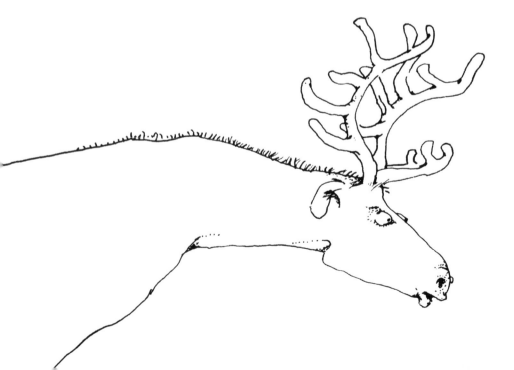

"I have games and toys for girls and boys,"
Said Santa cheerily.
The reindeer stood as if made of wood—
"But what do you have for me?"

"The socks are hung, the bells are rung!"
Cried Santa desperately.
The reindeer winked at a falling star—
"But what do you have for me?"

Then Santa reached into his beard,
And he found a tiny flea,
And he put it into the reindeer's ear,
And the reindeer said, "For me? Oh gee!"

And into the blue away they flew,
Away they flew with the flea.
And the moral of this yuletide tale
You know as well as me.

THE TOUCAN

Tell me who can
Catch a toucan?
Lou can.

Just how few can
Ride the toucan?
Two can.

What kind of goo can
Stick you to the toucan?
Glue can.

Who can write some
More about the toucan?
You can!

THE PLANET OF MARS

On the planet of Mars
They have clothes just like ours,
And they have the same shoes and same laces,
And they have the same charms and same graces,
And they have the same heads and same faces . . .
But not in the
Very same
Places.

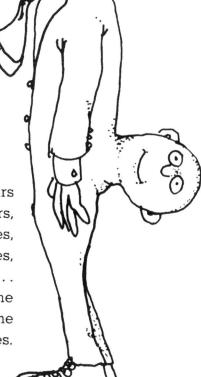

LOVE

Ricky was "L" but he's home with the flu,
Lizzie, our "O," had some homework to do,
Mitchell, "E" prob'ly got lost on the way,
So I'm all of love that could make it today.

THE DIRTIEST MAN IN THE WORLD

Oh I'm Dirty Dan, the world's dirtiest man,
I never have taken a shower.
I can't see my shirt—it's so covered with dirt,
And my ears have enough to grow flowers.

But the water is either a little too hot,
Or else it's a little too cold.
I'm musty and dusty and patchy and scratchy
And mangy and covered with mold.
But the water is always a little too hot,
Or else it's a little too cold.

I live in a pen with five hogs and a hen
And three squizzly lizards who creep in
My bed, and they itch as I squirm, and I twitch
In the cruddy old sheets that I sleep in.

If you looked down my throat with a flashlight, you'd note
That my insides are coated with rust.
I creak when I walk and I squeak when I talk,
And each time I sneeze I blow dust.

The thought of a towel and some soap makes me howl,
And when people have something to tell me
They don't come and tell it—they stand back and yell it.
I think they're afraid they might smell me.

The bedbugs that leap on me sing me to sleep,
And the garbage flies buzz me awake.
They're the best friends I've found and I fear they might drown
So I never go too near a lake.

Each evening at nine I sit down to dine
With the termites who live in my chair,
And I joke with the bats and have intimate chats
With the cooties who crawl through my hair.

I'd brighten my life if I just found a wife,
But I fear that that never will be
Until I can find a girl, gentle and kind,
With a beautiful face and a sensitive mind,
Who sparkles and twinkles and glistens and shines—
And who's almost as dirty as me.

POINT OF VIEW

Thanksgiving dinner's sad and thankless
Christmas dinner's dark and blue
When you stop and try to see it
From the turkey's point of view.

Sunday dinner isn't sunny
Easter feasts are just bad luck
When you see it from the viewpoint
Of a chicken or a duck.

Oh how I once loved tuna salad
Pork and lobsters, lamb chops too
Till I stopped and looked at dinner
From the dinner's point of view.

MAGICAL ERASER

She wouldn't believe
This pencil has
A magical eraser.
She said I was a silly moo,
She said I was a liar too,
She dared me prove that it was true,
And so what could I do—
I erased her!

SPAGHETTI

Spaghetti, spaghetti, all over the place,
Up to my elbows—up to my face,
Over the carpet and under the chairs,
Into the hammock and wound round the stairs,
Filling the bathtub and covering the desk,
Making the sofa a mad mushy mess.

The party is ruined, I'm terribly worried,
The guests have all left (unless they're all buried).
I told them, "Bring presents." I said, "Throw confetti."
I guess they heard wrong
'Cause they all threw spaghetti!

HELPING

Agatha Fry, she made a pie,
And Christopher John helped bake it.
Christopher John, he mowed the lawn,
And Agatha Fry helped rake it.
Zachary Zugg took out the rug,
And Jennifer Joy helped shake it.
And Jennifer Joy, she made a toy,
And Zachary Zugg helped break it.

And some kind of help
Is the kind of help
That helping's all about.
And some kind of help
Is the kind of help
We all can do without.

IF I HAD A BRONTOSAURUS

If I had a brontosaurus,
I would name him Horace or Morris.
But if suddenly one day he had
A lot of little brontosauri—
I would change his name
To Laurie.

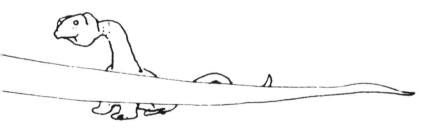

BENJAMIN BUNNN

Poor Benjamin Bunnn,
From Wilmington,
His buttons will not come undone.
He hasn't changed his clothes since last July.
And why?
'Cause no one can unbutton him
No matter how they try, poor guy.
And all that he can take off are his socks and shoes and tie,
And all that he can do is sit and bite his tongue and cry,
And he cannot take a bath—so just lets the water run,
And he can't go to the toilet, and he can't get any sun,
And life just isn't any fun
For Benjamin Bunnn, from Wilmington,
Whose buttons will not come undone.

THE BATTLE

Would you like to hear
Of the terrible night
When I bravely fought the—
No?
All right.

MINNOW MINNIE

May I ask you if you've noticed,
May I ask you if you've seen
My minnow Minnie
Who was swimmin'
In your Ovaltine?
For you've gone and drunk it up, dear,
And she isn't in the cup, dear,
And she's nowhere to be found, dear.
Do you think that she has drowned, dear?

THE RAZOR-TAILED WREN

The razor-tailed wren,
He'll pretend he's your friend
As he cuts all the grass on your lawn,
But do not leave anything
Sticking far out
Or swishity—it will be gone.

PLEASE
DO NOT
MAKE F
UN OF
ME AN
D PLEAS
E DON'T
LAUGH
IT ISN'T
EASY T
O WRIT
E A PO
EM ON
THE NE
CK OF
A RUN
NING
GIRA
FFE.

THE BLOATH

In the undergrowth
There dwells a Bloath
Who feeds upon poets and tea.
Luckily, I know this about him
While he knows almost nothing of me!

THE YIPIYUK

In the swamplands long ago,
Where the weeds and mudglumps grow,
A Yipiyuk bit on my toe . . .
Exactly why I do not know.
I kicked and cried
And hollered "Oh"—
The Yipiyuk would not let go.
I whispered to him soft and low—
The Yipiyuk would not let go.
I shouted "Stop," "Desist" and "Whoa"—
The Yipiyuk would not let go.
Yes, that was sixteen years ago,
And the Yipiyuk still won't let go.
The snow may fall,
The winds may blow—
The Yipiyuk will not let go.
The snow may melt,
The grass may grow—
The Yipiyuk will not let go.
I drag him 'round each place I go,
This Yipiyuk that won't let go.
And now my child at last you know
Exactly why I walk so slow.

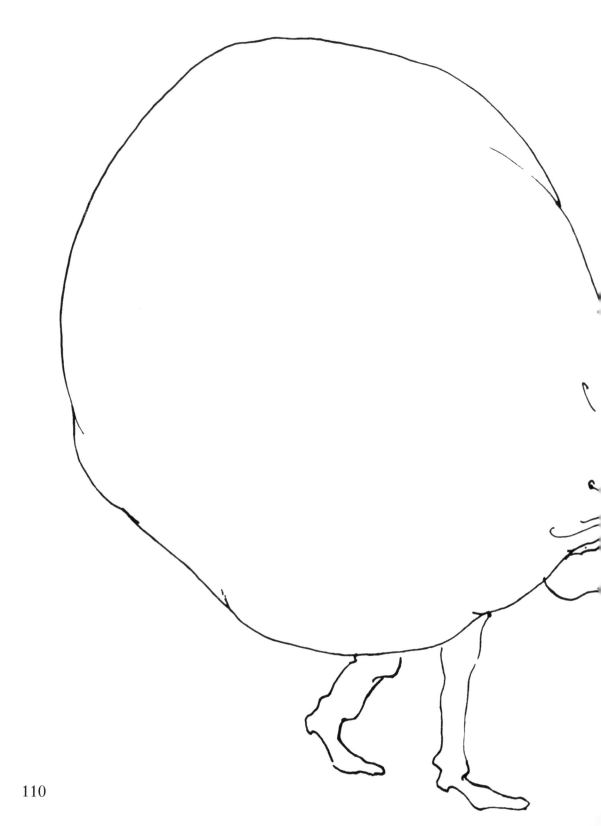

110

WHAT'S IN THE SACK?

What's in the sack? What's in the sack?
Is it some mushrooms or is it the moon?
Is it love letters or downy goosefeathers?
Or maybe the world's most enormous balloon?

What's in the sack? That's all they ask me.
Could it be popcorn or marbles or books?
Is it two years' worth of your dirty laundry,
Or the biggest ol' meatball that's ever been cooked?

Does anyone ask me, "Hey, when is your birthday?"
"Can you play Monopoly?" "Do you like beans?"
"What is the capital of Yugoslavia?"
Or "Who embroidered that rose on your jeans?"

No, what's in the sack? That's all they care about.
Is it a rock or a rolled-up giraffe?
Is it pickles or nickels or busted bicycles?
And if we guess it, will you give us half?

Do they ask where I've been, or how long I'll be stayin',
Where I'll be goin', or when I'll be back,
Or "How do?" or "What's new?" or "Hey, why are you blue?"
No, all they keep asking is, "What's in the sack?"
"What's in the sack?" I'm blowin' my stack
At the next one who asks me, "What's in the sack?"
What?
Oh no. Not you, too!

WON'T YOU?

Barbara's eyes are blue as azure
But she is in love with Freddy,
Karen's sweet but Harry has her,
Gentle Jane is going steady.
Carol hates me, so does May,
Abigail will not be mine,
Nancy lives too far away . . .
Won't you be my Valentine?

ALICE

She drank from a bottle called DRINK ME
And up she grew so tall,
She ate from a plate called TASTE ME
And down she shrank so small.
And so she changed, while other folks
Never tried nothin' at all.

SHADOW WASH

I've never washed my shadow out
In all the time I've had it.
It was absolutely filthy I supposed,
And so today I peeled it off
The wall where it was leaning
And stuck it in the washtub
With the clothes.
I put in soap and bleach and stuff,
I let it soak for hours,
I wrung it out and hung it out to dry,
And whoever would have thunk
That it would have gone and shrunk
For now it's so much
Littler than I.

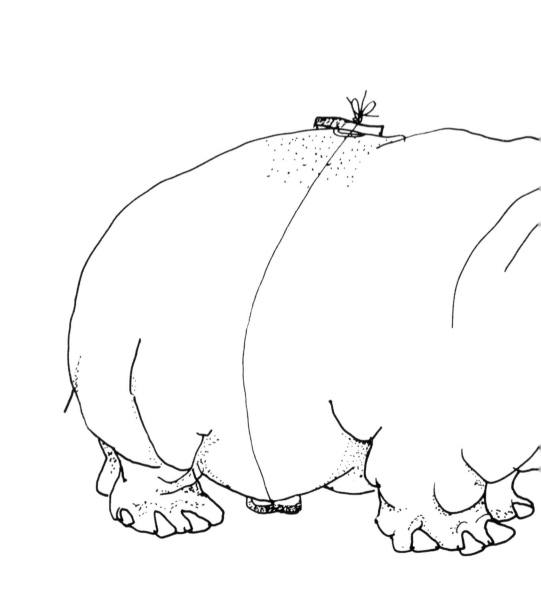

RECIPE FOR A
HIPPOPOTAMUS SANDWICH

A hippo sandwich is easy to make.
All you do is simply take
One slice of bread,
One slice of cake,
Some mayonnaise,
One onion ring,
One hippopotamus,
One piece of string,
A dash of pepper—
That ought to do it.
And now comes the problem . . .
Biting into it!

EIGHTEEN FLAVORS

Eighteen luscious, scrumptious flavors—
Chocolate, lime and cherry,
Coffee, pumpkin, fudge-banana,
Caramel cream and boysenberry,
Rocky road and toasted almond,
Butterscotch, vanilla dip,
Butter-brickle, apple ripple,
Coconut and mocha chip,
Brandy peach and lemon custard,
Each scoop lovely, smooth, and round,
Tallest ice-cream cone in town,
Lying there (sniff) on the ground.

POOR ANGUS

Oh what do you do, poor Angus,
When hunger makes you cry?
"I fix myself an omelet, sir,
Of fluffy clouds and sky."

Oh what do you wear, poor Angus,
When winds blow down the hills?
"I sew myself a warm cloak, sir,
Of hope and daffodils."

Oh who do you love, poor Angus,
When Catherine's left the moor?
"Ah, then, sir, then's the only time
I feel I'm really poor."

WHAT A DAY

What a day,
Oh what a day.
My baby brother ran away,
And now my tuba will not play.
I'm eight years old
And turning grey,
Oh what a day,
Oh what a day.

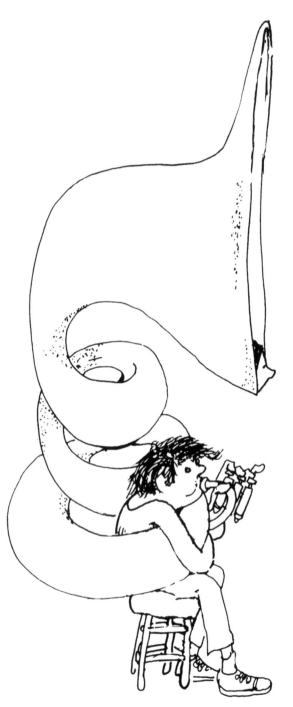

MA AND GOD

God gave us fingers—Ma says, "Use your fork."
God gave us voices—Ma says, "Don't scream."
Ma says eat broccoli, cereal and carrots.
But God gave us tasteys for maple ice cream.

God gave us fingers—Ma says, "Use your hanky."
God gave us puddles—Ma says, "Don't splash."
Ma says, "Be quiet, your father is sleeping."
But God gave us garbage can covers to crash.

God gave us fingers—Ma says, "Put your gloves on."
God gave us raindrops—Ma says, "Don't get wet."
Ma says be careful, and don't get too near to
Those strange lovely dogs that God gave us to pet.

God gave us fingers—Ma says, "Go wash 'em."
But God gave us coal bins and nice dirty bodies.
And I ain't too smart, but there's one thing for certain—
Either Ma's wrong or else God is.

BANG-KLANG

I'm Big Barney Zang of the railroad gang,
My partner is Charlie O'Flynn.
And I hold the nails
For the big steel rails,
And Charlie, he hammers 'em in.
And most of the time
He does just fine,
But now and again he fails.
Maybe tomorrow I'll hammer 'em in,
And let Charlie hold the nails.

TRAFFIC LIGHT

The traffic light simply would not turn green
So the people stopped to wait
As the traffic rolled and the wind blew cold
And the hour grew dark and late.

Zoom-varoom, trucks, trailers,
Bikes and limousines,
Clatterin' by—me oh my!
Won't that light turn green?

But the days turned weeks, and the weeks turned months
And there on the corner they stood,
Twiddlin' their thumbs till the changin' comes
The way good people should.

And if you walk by that corner now,
You may think it's rather strange
To see them there as they hopefully gaze
With the very same smile on their very same face
As they patiently stand in the very same place
And wait for the light to change.

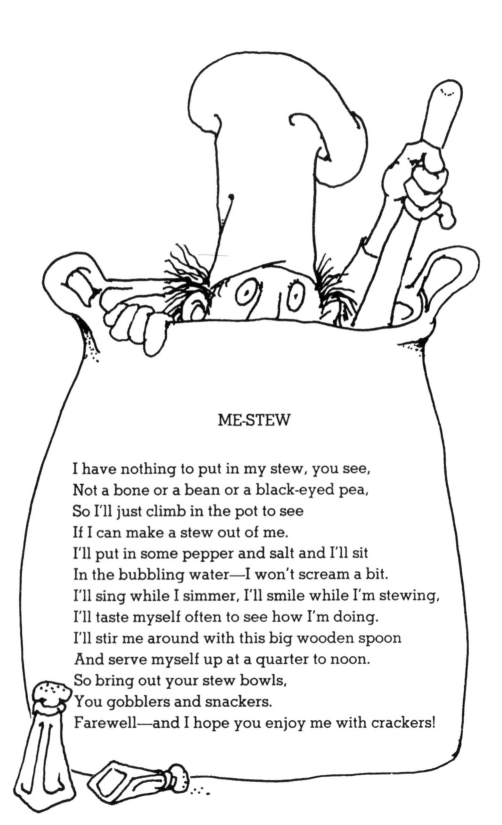

ME-STEW

I have nothing to put in my stew, you see,
Not a bone or a bean or a black-eyed pea,
So I'll just climb in the pot to see
If I can make a stew out of me.
I'll put in some pepper and salt and I'll sit
In the bubbling water—I won't scream a bit.
I'll sing while I simmer, I'll smile while I'm stewing,
I'll taste myself often to see how I'm doing.
I'll stir me around with this big wooden spoon
And serve myself up at a quarter to noon.
So bring out your stew bowls,
You gobblers and snackers.
Farewell—and I hope you enjoy me with crackers!

DOUBLE-TAIL DOG

Would you like to buy a dog with a tail at either end?
He is quite the strangest dog there is in town.
Though he's not too good at knowing
Just exactly where he's going,
He is very very good at sitting down.

He doesn't have a place to put a collar,
And I'll admit it's rather hard to lead him,
And he cannot hear you call
For he has no ears at all,
But it doesn't cost a single cent to feed him.

He cannot bite, he'll never bark or growl,
Just scratch him on his tails, he'll find it pleasing.
But you'll have to take him out
For twice as many walks,
And I'll bet that you can quickly guess the reason.

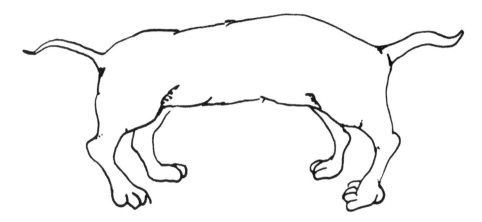

PAUL BUNYAN

He rode through the woods on a big blue ox,
He had fists as hard as choppin' blocks,
Five hundred pounds and nine feet tall . . . that's Paul.

Talk about workin', when he swung his axe
You could hear it ring for a mile and a half.
Then he'd yell "Timber!" and down she'd fall . . . for Paul.

Talk about drinkin', that man's so mean
That he'd never drink nothin' but kerosene,
And a five-gallon can is a little bit small . . . for Paul.

Talk about tough, well he once had a fight
With a thunderstorm on a cold dark night.
I ain't sayin' who won,
But it don't storm at all . . . 'round here . . . thanks to Paul.

He was ninety years old when he said with a sigh,
"I think I'm gonna lay right down and die
'Cause sunshine and sorrow, I've seen it all" . . . says Paul.

He says, "There ain't no man alive can kill me,
Ain't no woman 'round can thrill me,
And I think heaven just might be a ball" . . . says Paul.

So he died . . . and we cried.

It took eighteen men just to bust the ground,
It took twenty-four more just to lower him down.
And we covered him up and we figured that was all . . . for Paul.

But late one night the trees started shakin',
The dogs started howlin' and the earth started quakin',
And out of the ground with a "Hi, y'all" . . . come Paul!

He shook the dirt from off of his clothes,
He scratched his butt and he wiped his nose.
"Y'know, bein' dead wasn't no fun at all" . . . says Paul.

He says, "Up in heaven they got harps on their knees,
They got clouds and wings but they got no trees.
I don't think that's much of a heaven at all" . . . says Paul.

So he jumps on his ox with a fare-thee-well,
He says, "I'll find out if they's trees in hell."
And he rode away, and that was all . . . we ever seen . . . of **Paul**.

But the next time you hear a "Timber!" yell
That sounds like it's comin' from the pits of hell,
Then a weird and devilish ghostly wail
Like somebody choppin' on the devil's tail,
Then a shout, a call, a crash, a fall—
That ain't no mortal man at all . . . that's Paul!

DANCING PANTS

And now for the Dancing Pants,
Doing their fabulous dance.
From the seat to the pleat
They will bounce to the beat,
With no legs inside them
And no feet beneath.
They'll whirl, and twirl, and jiggle and prance,
So just start the music
And give them a chance—
Let's have a big hand for the wonderful, marvelous,
Super sensational, utterly fabulous,
Talented Dancing Pants!

I WON'T HATCH!

Oh I am a chickie who lives in an egg,
But I will not hatch, I will not hatch.
The hens they all cackle, the roosters all beg,
But I will not hatch, I will not hatch.
For I hear all the talk of pollution and war
As the people all shout and the airplanes roar,
So I'm staying in here where it's safe and it's warm,
And I WILL NOT HATCH!

WITH HIS MOUTH FULL OF FOOD

Milford Dupree, though he knew it was rude,
Talked with his mouth full of food.
He never would burp or walk out in the nude,
But he talked with his mouth full of food.
His mother said, "Milford, it's crude and it's lewd
To talk with your mouth full of food.
Why, even the milk cow who moo'd as she chewed
Never moo'd with her mouth full of food.
And the cuckoo would never have ever cuckoo'd
If he coo'd with his mouth full of food."
His dad said, "Get married or go get tattooed,
But don't talk with your mouth full of food.
If it was a crime, you would surely get sued
If you talked with your mouth full of food.
Why, just like an animal you should be zoo'd
As you talk with your mouth full of food.
For you know we're all put in a terrible mood
When you talk with your mouth full of food."
They pleaded and begged. He just giggled and chewed
And laughed with his mouth full of food.
And all they advised him he simply poo-poo'd,
He poo-poo'd with his mouth full of food.
So they sent for the gluer and had his mouth glued
'Cause he talked with his mouth full of food.
Now instead of "Good morning," he says "Gnu murnood,
I wun tuk win mny marf furu foog."

MY HOBBY

When you spit from the twenty-sixth floor,
And it floats on the breeze to the ground,
Does it fall upon hats
Or on white Persian cats
Or on heads, with a pitty-pat sound?
I used to think life was a bore,
But I don't feel that way anymore,
As I count up the hits,
As I smile as I sit,
As I spit from the twenty-sixth floor.

INSTRUCTIONS

If you should ever choose
To bathe an armadillo,
Use one bar of soap
And a whole lot of hope
And seventy-two pads of Brillo.

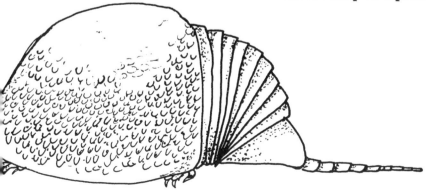

THE WORST

When singing songs of scariness,
Of bloodiness and hairyness,
I feel obligated at this moment to remind you
Of the most ferocious beast of all:
Three thousand pounds and nine feet tall—
The Glurpy Slurpy Skakagrall—
Who's standing right behind you.

THE BAGPIPE WHO DIDN'T SAY NO

It was nine o'clock at midnight at a quarter after three
When a turtle met a bagpipe on the shoreside by the sea,
And the turtle said, "My dearie,
May I sit with you? I'm weary."
And the bagpipe didn't say no.

Said the turtle to the bagpipe, "I have walked this lonely shore,
I have talked to waves and pebbles—but I've never loved before.
Will you marry me today, dear?
Is it 'No' you're going to say, dear?"
But the bagpipe didn't say no.

Said the turtle to his darling, "Please excuse me if I stare,
But you have the plaidest skin, dear,
And you have the strangest hair.
If I begged you pretty please, love,
Could I give you just one squeeze, love?"
And the bagpipe didn't say no.

Said the turtle to the bagpipe, "Ah, you love me. Then confess!
Let me whisper in your dainty ear and hold you to my chest."
And he cuddled her and teased her
And so lovingly he squeezed her.
And the bagpipe said, "Aaooga."

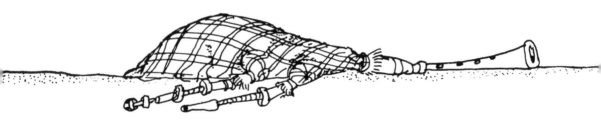

Said the turtle to the bagpipe, "Did you honk or bray or neigh?
For 'Aaooga' when you're kissed is such a heartless thing to say.
Is it that I have offended?
Is it that our love is ended?"
And the bagpipe didn't say no.

Said the turtle to the bagpipe, "Shall I leave you, darling wife?
Shall I waddle off to Woedom? Shall I crawl out of your life?
Shall I move, depart and go, dear—
Oh, I beg you tell me 'No,' dear!"
But the bagpipe didn't say no.

So the turtle crept off crying and he ne'er came back no more,
And he left the bagpipe lying on that smooth and sandy shore.
And some night when tide is low there,
Just walk up and say, "Hello, there,"
And politely ask the bagpipe if this story's really so.
I assure you, darling children, that the bagpipe won't say "No."

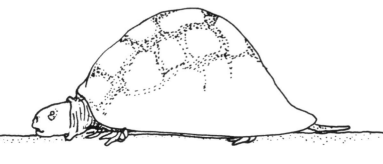

THE LONGEST NOSE IN THE WORLD, BELONGS

RUDY FELSH

Rudy Felsh
Knows how to belch
Better than anyone ever did.
Margo says that Rudy Felsh
Is a nasty vulgar kid.
Someday he will go to hell
Or jail or Canada, but now
Every night I pray that first
Rudy Felsh will show me how.

ISS BETSY BLUE BONNET-WHO LETS ME WRITE THINGS ON IT.

FRED?

From out of the cold Caribbean
Into the Desert Libyan
There crawled a strange amphibian,
And we shall call him "Fred."
You say let's call him "Ted"?
Or maybe "Lou" or "Jed"?
But I want to call him "Fred"!
You like "Maurice" instead?
Or "Barnaby" or "Red"
Or "Lucifer" or "Ned"?
Well, anyway, he's dead.

THE LONG-HAIRED BOY

There was a boy in our town with long hair—
I mean really long hair—
And everybody pointed at him
And laughed at him
And made fun of him.
And when he walked down the street
The people would roar
And stick their tongues out
And make funny faces
And run in and slam their door
And shout at him from the window
Until he couldn't stand it anymore.
So he sat down and cried
Till his whole body shook,
And pretty soon his hair shook too,
And it flapped
And flapped—
And he lifted—
And flew—

Straight up in the air like a helicopter.
Jenny Ricks saw him and dropped her
Knitting and screamed, "It's a flying kid!"
Lukey Hastings ran and hid
Under Old Man Merrill's car,
Miss Terance fainted, Henry Quist
Tried to shoot him down, but missed—
"I thought he was a crow," he said.
And 'round he sailed all through the day,
Smiling in the strangest way,
With the wind in his hair
And the sun in his eyes.
We saw him swoop and bank and rise.
He brushed the treetops
And skimmed the grass
On Yerbey's lawn and almost crashed
Right into Hansen's silo—but
Zoomed up in time and almost hit
The courthouse. Old Man Cooley bit
Right through his napkin when he saw
A kid fly through the diner door—
And out of the window, tipping the ladder—

Where Smokey was painting, he almost had a
Heart attack—he clung to a rafter.
The kid flew on—
Us runnin' after,
Cheering and sweating
And screaming, "Hooray!"
Mayor Lowry shouted, "Hey—
Come down here, kid. We'd like to say
How proud of you we are today.
Who ever thought our little
Town would have a hero in it?
So I'd like to proclaim this day—hey, kid!
Will you please come down for just a minute?"
But the flying kid did not come down.
He treaded air above the town,
Sort of cryin' and looking down
At all of us here on the ground.
Then up he flew, up into the clouds,
Flapping and flying so far and high,
Out past the hills and into the sky
Until a tiny speck against the sun
Was all we could see of him . . . then he was gone.

BAND-AIDS

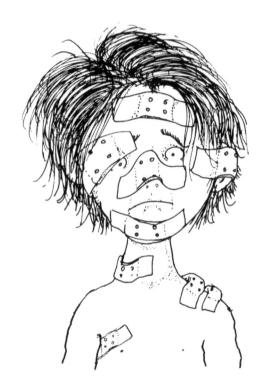

I have a Band-Aid on my finger,
One on my knee, and one on my nose,
One on my heel, and two on my shoulder,
Three on my elbow, and nine on my toes.
Two on my wrist, and one on my ankle,
One on my chin, and one on my thigh,
Four on my belly, and five on my bottom,
One on my forehead, and one on my eye.
One on my neck, and in case I might need 'em
I have a box full of thirty-five more.
But oh! I do think it's sort of a pity
I don't have a cut or a sore!

DREADFUL

Someone ate the baby,
It's rather sad to say.
Someone ate the baby
So she won't be out to play.
    We'll never hear her whiney cry
    Or have to feel if she is dry.
    We'll never hear her asking "Why?"
    Someone ate the baby.

Someone ate the baby.
It's absolutely clear
Someone ate the baby
'Cause the baby isn't here.
    We'll give away her toys and clothes.
    We'll never have to wipe her nose.
    Dad says, "That's the way it goes."
    Someone ate the baby.

Someone ate the baby.
What a frightful thing to eat!
Someone ate the baby
Though she wasn't very sweet.
    It was a heartless thing to do.
    The policemen haven't got a clue.
    I simply can't imagine who
    Would go and (burp) eat the baby.

SKINNY

Skinny McGuinn
was so terribly thin
that while taking his bath
Sunday night,
out popped the plug
and sloosh-swoosh
and glug-glug
it washed Skinny
right down the drain
out of sight.
And where is our dear Skinny
bathing tonight?
In some underground pool
down below?
Or up there so high
in that tub in the sky
where all of
the clean people go?

THE LAND OF HAPPY

Have you been to The Land of Happy,
Where everyone's happy all day,
Where they joke and they sing
Of the happiest things,
And everything's jolly and gay?
There's no one unhappy in Happy,
There's laughter and smiles galore.
I have been to The Land of Happy—
What a bore!

PIRATE CAPTAIN JIM

"Walk the plank," says Pirate Jim.
"But Captain Jim, I cannot swim."
"Then you must steer us through the gale."
"But Captain Jim, I cannot sail."
"Then down with the galley slaves you go."
"But Captain Jim, I cannot row."
"Then you must be the pirate's clerk."
"But Captain Jim, I cannot work."
"Then a pirate captain you must be."
"Thank you, Jim," says Captain Me.

FISH?

The little fish eats the tiny fish,
The big fish eats the little fish—
So only the biggest fish get fat.
Do you know any folks like that?

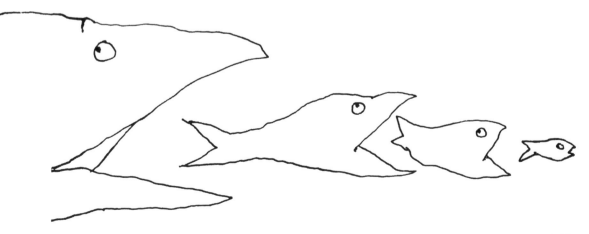

IF THE WORLD WAS CRAZY

If the world was crazy, you know what I'd eat?
A big slice of soup and a whole quart of meat,
A lemonade sandwich, and then I might try
Some roasted ice cream or a bicycle pie,
A nice notebook salad, an underwear roast,
An omelet of hats and some crisp cardboard toast,
A thick malted milk made from pencils and daisies,
And that's what I'd eat if the world was crazy.

If the world was crazy, you know what I'd wear?
A chocolate suit and a tie of éclair,
Some marshmallow earmuffs, some licorice shoes,
And I'd read a paper of peppermint news.
I'd call the boys "Suzy" and I'd call the girls "Harry,"
I'd talk through my ears, and I always would carry
A paper umbrella for when it grew hazy
To keep in the rain, if the world was crazy.

If the world was crazy, you know what I'd do?
I'd walk on the ocean and swim in my shoe,
I'd fly through the ground and I'd skip through the air,
I'd run down the bathtub and bathe on the stair.
When I met somebody I'd say "G'bye, Joe,"
And when I was leaving—then I'd say "Hello."
And the greatest of men would be silly and lazy
So I would be king . . . if the world was crazy.

STONE TELLING

How do we tell if a window is open?
Just throw a stone at it.
Does it make a noise?
It doesn't?
Well, it was open.
Now let's try another . . .
CRASH!
It wasn't!

CHESTER

Chester come to school and said,
"Durn, I growed another head."
Teacher said, "It's time you knowed
The word is 'grew' instead of 'growed.' "

THE SILVER FISH

While fishing in the blue lagoon
I caught a lovely silver fish,
And he spoke to me. "My boy," quoth he,
"Please set me free and I'll grant your wish . . .
A kingdom of wisdom? A palace of gold?
Or all the goodies your fancies can hold?"
So I said, "OK," and I threw him free,
And he swam away and he laughed at me
Whispering my foolish wish
Into a silent sea.
Today I caught that fish again,
That lovely silver prince of fishes,
And once again he offered me—
If I would only set him free—
Any one of a number of wonderful wishes. . . .
He was delicious!

FORGOTTEN LANGUAGE

Once I spoke the language of the flowers,
Once I understood each word the caterpillar said,
Once I smiled in secret at the gossip of the starlings,
And shared a conversation with the housefly
          in my bed.
Once I heard and answered all the questions
          of the crickets,
And joined the crying of each falling dying
          flake of snow,
Once I spoke the language of the flowers . . . .
          How did it go?
          How did it go?

THE GENERALS

Said General Clay to General Gore,
"Oh must we fight this silly war?
To kill and die is such a bore."
"I quite agree," said General Gore.

Said General Gore to General Clay,
"We could go to the beach today
And have some ice cream on the way."
"A grand idea," said General Clay.

Said General Clay to General Gore,
"We'll build sand castles on the shore."
Said General Gore, "We'll splash and play."
"Let's leave right now," said General Clay.

Said General Gore to General Clay,
"But what if the sea is closed today?
And what if the sand's been blown away?"
"A dreadful thought," said General Clay.

Said General Gore to General Clay,
"I've always feared the ocean's spray,
And we may drown!" "It's true, we may.
It chills my blood," said General Clay.

Said General Clay to General Gore,
"My bathing suit is slightly tore.
We'd better go on with our war."
"I quite agree," said General Gore.

Then General Clay charged General Gore
As bullets flew and cannons roared.
And now, alas! there is no more
Of General Clay or General Gore.

JUST ME, JUST ME

Sweet Marie, she loves just me
(She also loves Maurice McGhee).
No she don't, she loves just me
(She also loves Louise Dupree).
No she don't, she loves just me
(She also loves the willow tree).
No she don't, she loves just me!
(Poor, poor fool, why can't you see
She can love others and still love thee.)

STANDING

Standing on my elbow
With my finger in my ear,
Biting on a dandelion,
And humming kind of queer
While I watched a yellow caterpillar
Creeping up my wrist,
I leaned on a tree
And I said to me,
"Why am I doing this?"

THE ONE WHO STAYED

You should have heard the old men cry,
You should have heard the biddies
When that sad stranger raised his flute
And piped away the kiddies.
Katy, Tommy, Meg and Bob
Followed, skipping gaily,
Red-haired Ruth, my brother Rob,
And little crippled Bailey,
John and Nils and Cousin Claire,
Dancin', spinnin', turnin'
'Cross the hills to God knows where—
They never came returnin'.
'Cross the hills to God knows where
The piper pranced, a leadin'
Each child in Hamlin Town but me,
And I stayed home unheedin'.
My papa says that I was blest
For if that music found me,
I'd be witch-cast like all the rest.
This town grows old around me.
I cannot say I did not hear
That sound so haunting hollow—
I heard, I heard, I heard it clear . . .
I was afraid to follow.

MELINDA MAE

Have you heard of tiny Melinda Mae,
Who ate a monstrous whale?
She thought she could,
She said she would,
So she started in right at the tail.

And everyone said, "You're much too small,"
But that didn't bother Melinda at all.
She took little bites and she chewed very slow,
Just like a good girl should . . .

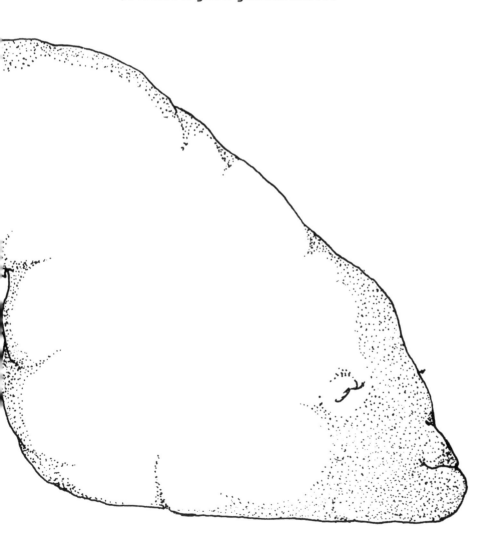

... And in eighty-nine years she ate that whale
Because she said she would!

THE LITTLE BLUE ENGINE

The little blue engine looked up at the hill.
His light was weak, his whistle was shrill.
He was tired and small, and the hill was tall,
And his face blushed red as he softly said,
"I think I can, I think I can, I think I can."

So he started up with a chug and a strain,
And he puffed and pulled with might and main.
And slowly he climbed, a foot at a time,
And his engine coughed as he whispered soft,
"I think I can, I think I can, I think I can."

With a squeak and a creak and a toot and a sigh,
With an extra hope and an extra try,
He would not stop—now he neared the top—
And strong and proud he cried out loud,
"I think I can, I think I can, I think I can!"

He was almost there, when—*CRASH! SMASH! BASH!*
He slid down and mashed into engine hash
On the rocks below . . . which goes to show
If the track is tough and the hill is rough,
THINKING you can just ain't enough!

AFRAID OF THE DARK

I'm Reginald Clark, I'm afraid of the dark
So I always insist on the light on,
And my teddy to hug,
And my blanket to rub,
And my thumby to suck or to bite on.
And three bedtime stories,
Two trips to the toilet,
Two prayers, and five hugs from my mommy,
I'm Reginald Clark, I'm afraid of the dark
So please do not close this book on me.

HUNGRY MUNGRY

Hungry Mungry sat at supper,
Took his knife and spoon and fork,
Ate a bowl of mushroom soup, ate a slice of roasted pork,
Ate a dozen stewed tomatoes, twenty-seven deviled eggs,
Fifteen shrimps, nine baked potatoes,
Thirty-two fried chicken legs,
A shank of lamb, a boiled ham,
Two bowls of grits, some black-eye peas,
Four chocolate shakes, eight angel cakes,
Nine custard pies with Muenster cheese,
Ten pots of tea, and after he
Had eaten all that he was able,
He poured some broth on the tablecloth
And ate the kitchen table.

His parents said, "Oh Hungry Mungry, stop these silly jokes."
Mungry opened up his mouth, and "Gulp," he ate his folks.
And then he went and ate his house, all the bricks and wood,
And then he ate up all the people in the neighborhood.
Up came twenty angry policemen shouting, "Stop and cease."
Mungry opened up his mouth and "Gulp," he ate the police.
Soldiers came with tanks and guns.
Said Mungry, "They can't harm me."
He just smiled and licked his lips and ate the U.S. Army.

The President sent all his bombers—Mungry still was calm,
Put his head back, gulped the planes, and gobbled up the bomb.
He ate his town and ate the city—ate and ate and ate—
And then he said, "I think I'll eat the whole United States."

And so he ate Chicago first and munched the Water Tower,
And then he chewed on Pittsburgh but he found it rather sour.
He ate New York and Tennessee, and all of Boston town,
Then drank the Mississippi River just to wash it down.
And when he'd eaten every state, each puppy, boy and girl
He wiped his mouth upon his sleeve and went to eat the world.

He ate the Egypt pyramids and every church in Rome,
And all the grass in Africa and all the ice in Nome.
He ate each hill in green Brazil and then to make things worse
He decided for dessert he'd eat the universe.

He started with the moon and stars and soon as he was done
He gulped the clouds, he sipped the wind and gobbled up the sun.
Then sitting there in the cold dark air,
He started to nibble his feet,
Then his legs, then his hips
Then his neck, then his lips
Till he sat there just gnashin' his teeth
'Cause nothin' was nothin' was
Nothin' was nothin' was
Nothin' was left to eat.

MY BEARD

My beard grows to my toes,
I never wears no clothes,
I wraps my hair
Around my bare,
And down the road I goes.

MERRY . . .

No one's hangin' stockin's up,
No one's bakin' pie,
No one's lookin' up to see
A new star in the sky.
No one's talkin' brotherhood,
No one's givin' gifts,
And no one loves a Christmas tree
On March the twenty-fifth.

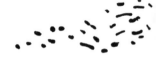

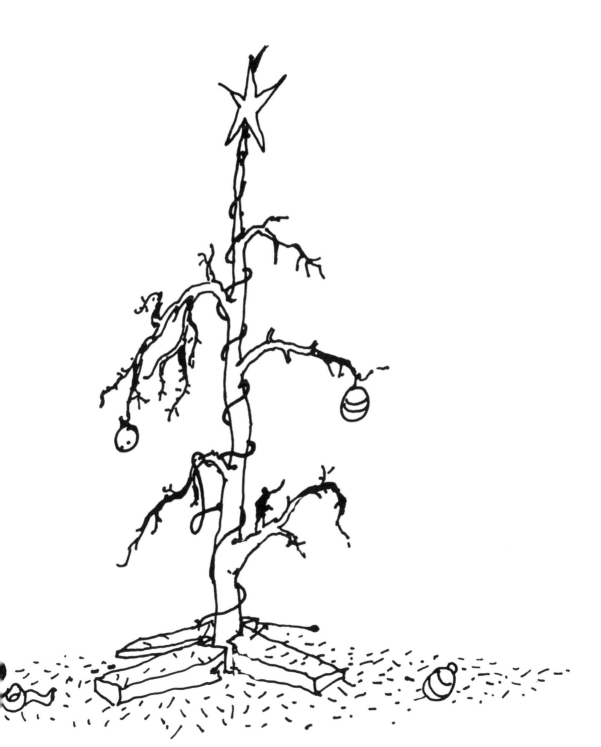

THE SEARCH

I went to find the pot of gold
That's waiting where the rainbow ends.
I searched and searched and searched and searched
And searched and searched, and then—
There it was, deep in the grass,
Under an old and twisty bough.
It's mine, it's mine, it's mine at last. . . .
What do I search for now?

Where the Sidewalk Ends

30th Anniversary
Special Edition Poems

THE TRUTH ABOUT TURTLES

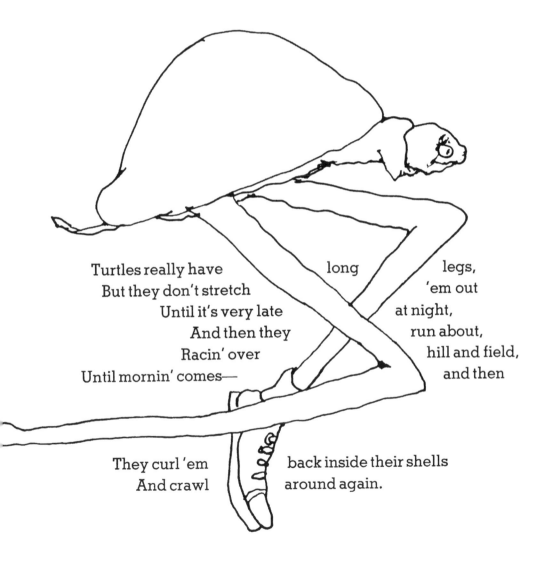

Turtles really have   long   legs,
  But they don't stretch   'em out
    Until it's very late   at night,
      And then they   run about,
        Racin' over   hill and field,
Until mornin' comes—   and then

  They curl 'em   back inside their shells
    And crawl   around again.

OOPS!

Down
Upside
Out
Come
All
Poems
My

Found
I
Can't
But
Try
Do
I

Around
All
Them
Turn
Not
Can
I

Down
Upside
Out
Come
All
Poems
My

MR. GRUMPLEDUMP'S SONG

Everything's wrong,
Days are too long,
Sunshine's too hot,
Wind is too strong.
Clouds are too fluffy,
Grass is too green,
Ground is too dusty,
Sheets are too clean.
Stars are too twinkly,
Moon is too high,
Water's too drippy,
Sand is too dry.
Rocks are too heavy,
Feathers too light,
Kids are too noisy,
Shoes are too tight.
Folks are too happy
Singin' their songs.
Why can't they see it?
Everything's wrong!

NAKED HIPPO

Let us make a pair of pants
For the poor old Hippopotamus
To cover his hide—once we decide
Exactly how big his bottomus.

173

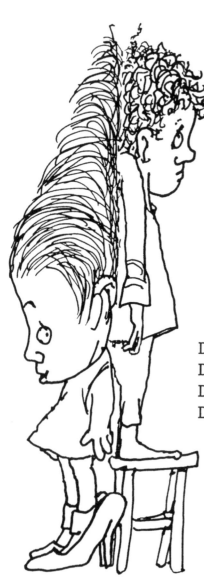

WHO'S TALLER?

Depends on if the judge is fair,
Depends how high the heels you wear,
Depends on if they count the hair,
Depends if they allow the chair.

MONSTERS

"There are hungry monsters under my bed,
Growlin' at me 'cause they haven't been fed."
That's what Harry McGilly said.
His father just smiled and said,
"Ho-ho-ho, fraidy-cat Harry,
Monsters are just imaginary."
But Harry McGilly cried out all night,
"There are hungry monsters—I know I'm right."
So just to prove that Harry was silly,
Under the bed crawled Mr. McGilly.
Harry heard a "chomp," he heard a "slurp,"
He heard a "gulp," he heard a "burp."
And now little Harry sleeps sound in his bed,
'Cause there are no monsters, as father said.
(And if there are—well—they've been fed.)

WEIGHTLIFTRESS

Nancy Bates can lift those weights
As well as any feller.
If you don't think it's ladylike,
Then you go up and tell her!

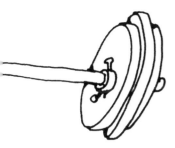

DON'T TELL ME

Please don't tell me I should hug,
Don't tell me I should care.
Don't tell me just how grand I'd feel
If I just learned to share.
Don't say, "It's all right to cry,"
"Be kind," "Be fair," "Be true."
Just let me see *YOU* do it,
Then I just might do it too.

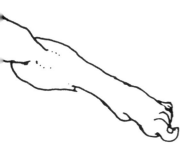

TEN-O-CYCLE

You pedal, you pump,
You bump on your rump,
You're sweatin' and ready to cuss,
When you're ridin' a bicycle built for ten
(And the other nine took the bus).

THE UNFUNNY JESTER

The jester told a silly joke,
The king just frowned—nobody spoke.
The jester sang a funny song,
The queen asked, "Must it last so long?"
The jester did a funny leap,
The prince and princess fell asleep.
The king looked mad and asked the Fool,
"Have you been to Funny School?"
"Yes," said the jester—and hesitated . . .
"But I never graduated."

OPEN—CLOSE

Open your mouth and close your eyes
And you might get a big surprise.
It might be a cake made with sugar and spice,
It might be two blueberry whipped cream pies,
It might be a basket of crispy French fries,
It might be those muffins your grandmother buys.
But wouldn't it be a bit more wise
To *close* your *mouth*—and *open* your eyes.

GORILLA

Since I brought my gorilla to school,
Everyone's nicer to me.
The teacher's more pleasant,
The kids bring me presents,
The principal serves me
Bran muffins and tea.

If I'm tardy, they say, "Oh, don't worry."
If I'm absent, they don't give a hoot.
If my desk is a mess or I'm sloppily dressed
Or I snooze on my desk,
Or I cheat on a test, they say,
"Isn't that cute."

If I don't know my lessons,
I just take a guess and whatever I guess,
Teacher screams out, "That's right!"
And big bully Slick
Has been stayin' home sick,
Afraid that I'll trick him right into a fight.

I'm welcome to munch upon anyone's lunch,
And I was just voted "Most clever and cool."
Though I chew gum and play,
My report card's all As
Since the day I first brought
My gorilla to school.

INDEX

The work and love of many people
went into the making of this book.
To Ursula Nordstrom, Barbara Borack,
Dorothy Hagen, Beri Greenwald,
and Gloria Bressler... and to Bill Cole
for his continued encouragement... Thank you.

ACKNOWLEDGMENTS

*The following poems have been published previously in
slightly different versions:*

"I Must Remember," "Flag," and "Oh Have You Heard" previously appeared in *Poems for Seasons and Celebrations* edited by William Cole. Copyright © 1961 by William Cole. World Publishing Company. "Oh Have You Heard" previously appeared as "Oh Did You Hear?"

"Early Bird" first appeared in *Poetry Brief* edited by William Cole. Copyright © 1971 by William Cole. The Macmillan Company. The poem also appeared in lyric form. © Copyright 1973 Evil Eye Music, Inc., New York, New York. Used by permission.

"Rain," "For Sale," "Tight Hat," "If I Had a Brontosaurus," and "The Generals" previously appeared in *Oh, That's Ridiculous!* Poems selected by William Cole. Text copyright © 1972 by William Cole. The Viking Press, Inc. "The Generals" also appeared in lyric form as "The Peace Proposal." © Copyright 1972 Evil Eye Music, Inc., New York, New York. Used by permission.

"Boa Constrictor" first appeared in lyric form. TRO – © Copyright 1962, 1968, and 1969 by Hollis Music, Inc., New York, New York. Used by permission. "Boa Constrictor" also appeared in *Oh, What Nonsense!* Poems selected by William Cole. Text copyright © 1966 by William Cole. The Viking Press, Inc.

"Invention" and "My Rules" previously appeared in *Pick Me Up: A Book of Short Poems* edited by William Cole. Copyright © 1972 by William Cole. The Macmillan Company.

"Sarah Cynthia Sylvia Stout Would Not Take the Garbage Out" first appeared in *Beastly Boys and Ghastly Girls* edited by William Cole. Copyright © 1964 by William Cole. World Publishing Company. The poem also appeared in lyric form as "Sahra Cynthia Sylvia Stout Would Not Take the Garbage Out." © Copyright 1973 Evil Eye Music, Inc., New York, New York. Used by permission.

"Drats" previously appeared as "Wanted" in *A Cat-Hater's Handbook or the Ailurophobe's Delight* edited by William Cole and Tomi Ungerer. Copyright © 1963 by William Cole and Tomi Ungerer. The Dial Press, Inc.

"The Unicorn" and "The Flying Festoon" previously appeared in lyric form. TRO – © Copyright 1962 and 1968 Hollis Music, Inc., New York, New York. Used by permission.

"Helping" first appeared in lyric form in *Free To Be . . . You and Me*. Copyright © 1972 by The Ms. Foundation for Women, Inc. The poem also appeared in *Free To Be . . . You and Me*. Copyright © 1974, Free to be Foundation, Inc. McGraw-Hill Book Company.

"The Bloath" previously appeared as "About the Bloath" in *The Birds and the Beasts Were There* edited by William Cole. Copyright © 1963 by William Cole. World Publishing Company.

"Won't You?" previously appeared as an untitled poem in *A Book of Love Poems* edited by William Cole. Copyright © 1965 by William Cole. The Viking Press, Inc.

"Paul Bunyan" previously appeared in lyric form. © Copyright 1968, 1969 Evil Eye Music, Inc., New York, New York. Used by permission.

"The Silver Fish" previously appeared in *The Sea, Ships and Sailors: Poems, Songs and Shanties* selected by William Cole. Copyright © 1967 by William Cole. The Viking Press, Inc.

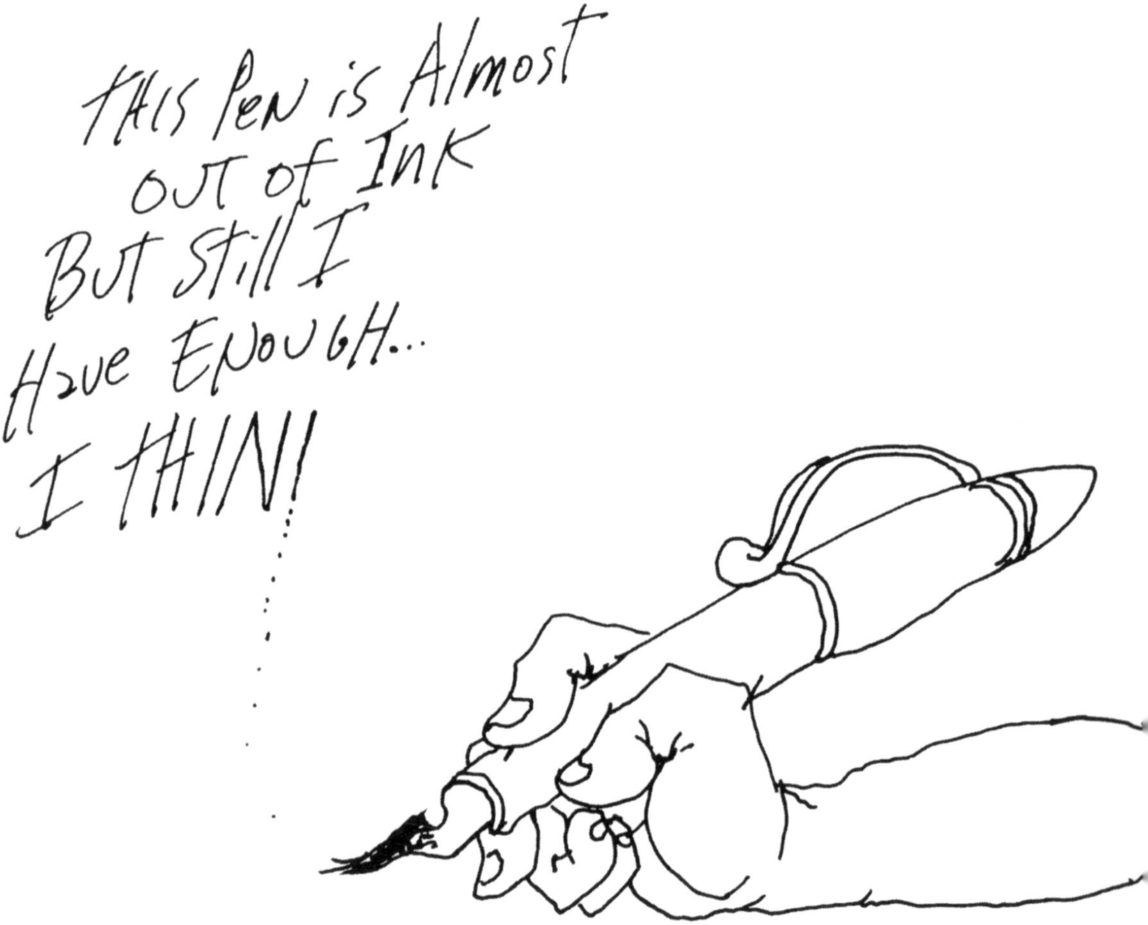
This Pen is Almost
out of Ink
But Still I
Have Enough...
I THIN